Preface

As a mother of three children, I have had the pleasure of planning and executing many birthday parties over the years. From my first-born's first birthday to my youngest child's most recent milestone at 15, each party has held a special place in my heart.

As I sit down to write this book, I am filled with fond memories of the laughter, joy, and love that have surrounded each and every celebration. I remember the excitement of planning my first-born's first birthday party. I spent weeks researching themes and party favors, trying to make it the perfect day for my little one. I remember the thrill of seeing the look of wonder on his face as he took in all the decorations and balloons. It was a small gathering of family and close friends, but it was one of the most memorable days of my life.

As my children grew older, so did the parties. Each year brought new challenges and opportunities to create something special. I remember my daughter's fifth birthday party, where we had a tea party theme complete with miniature sandwiches and a homemade cake. The look of delight on her face as she sat at the head of the table, surrounded by her friends, was priceless.

As my children entered their teenage years, I found myself reminiscing about the simpler days of the past. However, I quickly realized that the joy and excitement of planning a party never fades, no matter the age of the child. My son's 15th birthday party was a perfect example of this. We planned a surprise camping trip with his closest friends and the memories made that weekend will stay with all of us forever.

I know that planning a child's birthday party can be overwhelming and stressful, especially when you want everything to be perfect. That's why I've put together this guide to help other moms like me. This book has ten chapters, with each chapter focusing on each age, until the child turns 10. Each chapter will provide you with ideas for themes, party favors, decorations, and more. I'll also share my personal experience and advice on how to plan a memorable and stress-free celebration for your child.

I'll take you through the first birthday all the way to the tenth, each milestone is special and should be celebrated in a unique and meaningful way. I'll give you advice on how to make the party special and memorable for your child, and how to make it nostalgic and delightful for you as well. I'll help you to create a celebration that will be cherished by your child forever, and that your family and friends will talk about for years to come.

I hope that my story and advice will inspire you to create memories that will last a lifetime for your little one, just like it has for mine. I hope this guide will be a helpful and valuable resource for you as you plan and execute birthday parties for your child.

I know that being a mom is hard, and finding the time to plan a party can be overwhelming. But, I assure you that with this guide, you'll be able to plan and execute the perfect party for your child with ease and confidence. I hope that this book will bring you the same joy and excitement that planning my children's birthday parties have brought me over the years.

CHAPTER ONE
One-Of-A-Kind-Party

As a mother, there's nothing more exciting than planning your child's first birthday party. It's a special milestone that marks the first year of your child's life and it's a time to celebrate with family and friends. But, let's be real, planning your baby's first birthday party can also be overwhelming and stressful.

When planning your child's first birthday party, the guest list is one of the first things to consider. This is a special milestone for your child and you'll want to share it with loved ones, but keep in mind that it's a first birthday party so you don't need to invite everyone you know. A smaller gathering of close family and friends is more than enough.

It's important to remember that this is your child's first birthday and the focus should be on them, not on impressing others. A smaller guest list will allow you to focus on your child and create a more intimate and enjoyable experience for everyone. It will also make it easier to plan and execute the party.

Next, you'll want to decide on a theme for the party. This is the perfect time to let your creativity shine. Some popular themes for 1st birthday parties include: animals, jungle, under the sea, teddy bears and many more. Don't be afraid to get creative and think outside the box.

When choosing a theme for your child's first birthday party, it's important to consider your child's interests and personality. If your child loves animals, a zoo or jungle-themed party would be perfect. If they love the ocean, an under the sea-themed party would be a great option. The theme should reflect your child and make them feel special.

When it comes to decorations, you don't need to go all out. Keep it simple and elegant. A few balloons, streamers, and a homemade banner with your child's name and age will do the trick. Remember, the focus should be on the birthday baby, not the decorations.

When decorating for your child's first birthday party, less is more. You don't want to overwhelm your guests or your child with too many decorations. Instead, keep it simple and elegant with a few balloons, streamers, and a homemade banner with your child's name and age.

Food is another important aspect of the party. Keep in mind that most of your guests will be adults, so you'll want to have a mix of adult and kid-friendly food. Finger foods and snacks are a great option for this age group. You can also consider hiring a caterer or having a potluck with friends and family.

When planning the food for your child's first birthday party, it's important to keep in mind that most of the guests will be adults, and they will be expecting more than just plain snacks or finger foods. You can offer a mix of savory and sweet options like mini sandwiches, quiche, cheese and crackers, and cupcakes. This will ensure that all of your guests are satisfied and happy.

The cake is also a significant part of the celebration, and a delicious and beautifully decorated cake is a must-have. If you're not comfortable making a cake, you can always order one from a bakery or have a friend or family member make one for you.

The cake is one of the highlights of any birthday party, and your child's first birthday is no exception. It's important to have a delicious and beautifully decorated cake to mark this special milestone. You can choose a cake that complements your party theme or something that your child likes. If you're not comfortable making a cake, you can always order one from a bakery or have a friend or family member make one for you.

For entertainment, you don't need to go all out. Simple activities like a sing-along, a photo booth, or a bubble machine will keep the little ones entertained.

When it comes to entertainment, keep in mind that this is a first birthday party, and the focus should be on the birthday baby and their enjoyment. Simple activities like a sing-along, a photo booth, or a bubble machine will keep the little ones entertained without.

Finally, don't forget the party favors. This is a great way to thank your guests for coming and to remind them of the special day. Favors can be as simple as a small bag of sweets or a homemade craft.

When it comes to party favors, it's important to keep it simple and age-appropriate. For a first birthday party, you can give out small bags of sweets or homemade crafts like a picture frame with a photo of the birthday baby or a small plant in a pot. These favors are a great way to thank your guests for coming and to remind them of the special day.

In conclusion, planning and executing a 1st birthday party can be overwhelming, but it doesn't have to be. Keep it simple, focus on the birthday baby, and enjoy the special day with your loved ones. Remember, it's not about the extravagance of the party, it's about the memories you'll create and cherish forever. As a mother, I understand the excitement and stress that comes with planning a 1st birthday party. But, I can tell you from experience, the end result is worth all the effort. So, take a deep breath, relax, and enjoy the planning process. You and your little one will have the time of your life.

CHAPTER TWO
Two Much Fun

The second birthday is a special milestone for your child and a time to celebrate with family and friends. By this age, your child is becoming more aware of their surroundings and is beginning to understand the concept of birthdays and parties. This means that the planning and execution of the party will be a little more challenging than the first one, but it also opens up new opportunities for themes, decorations, and activities.

When planning your child's second birthday party, the guest list is still an important consideration. You can invite a little more people than the first birthday, but keep in mind that your child may not be able to handle a large gathering of people. A small group of family and close friends is still a good idea.

As your child is becoming more aware of their surroundings, you can choose a theme that reflects their interests and personality. Popular themes for 2nd birthday parties include: favorite characters, colors, and toys. For example, if your child loves Thomas the Tank Engine, you can have a train-themed party. If they love the color pink, you can have a pink-themed party.

When it comes to decorations, you can be a little more elaborate than the first birthday party. You can include more balloons, streamers, and decorations that match the theme of the party. You can also add more interactive elements like a photo booth or a DIY craft station.

Food is still an important aspect of the party. You can offer a mix of adult and kid-friendly food, but also consider incorporating some finger foods that your child can try and enjoy. The cake is still a significant part of the celebration, and you can choose a cake that matches the theme of the party or one that your child loves.

For entertainment, you can include more interactive activities that match the theme of the party. For example, if you have a train-themed party, you can include a train ride for the children. If it's a pink-themed party, you can have a bubble machine or a pink piñata. You can also consider hiring a professional entertainer like a clown or a magician to keep the children entertained.

Finally, don't forget the party favors. You can choose favors that match the theme of the party or something that your child likes. For example, if it's a train-themed party, you can give out small toy trains as favors. If it's a pink-themed party, you can give out pink-themed crafts or candies.

Don't forget to also consider the logistics of the party such as the location, timing and any special accommodations that may be required. You should also consider the timing of the party, as a 2-year-old's attention span and energy levels may not be able to handle a long party. Also, consider hiring a professional photographer to capture all the memories of this special milestone.

When planning your child's 2nd birthday party, it's important to keep in mind that your child is becoming more aware of their surroundings and is beginning to understand the concept of birthdays and parties. This means that you'll need to make the party more interactive and engaging for them.

In conclusion, planning and executing a 2nd birthday party can be a little more challenging than the first one, but it also opens up new opportunities for themes, decorations, and activities. Remember to keep the guest list small, choose a theme that reflects your child's interests and personality, and include interactive elements and activities to keep the children entertained. With a little bit of planning, attention to detail and a lot of love, you'll be able to create a special and memorable celebration for your child.

CHAPTER THREE
Third Time's Charm

The third birthday marks a significant milestone in your child's life as they begin to understand the concept of friendships and socializing. This means that your child's third birthday party should be geared towards interactive activities, games, and fun.

When planning your child's third birthday party, it's important to keep in mind that your child is now more aware of their surroundings and may have specific interests or preferences. You can use this as an opportunity to plan a themed party that reflects your child's interests. Popular themes for 3rd birthday parties include: superheroes, dinosaurs, princesses and many more.

When it comes to decorations, you can be a bit more elaborate than the previous years, but still keep it age-appropriate. Balloons, streamers, and decorations that match the theme of the party are always a hit. You can also consider adding interactive elements like a bounce house, a face painting station, or a piñata.

Food is still an important aspect of the party, and you can offer a mix of adult and kid-friendly food. You can also consider incorporating a candy buffet or a dessert table to add an extra special touch. The cake is still a significant part of the celebration, and you can choose a cake that matches the theme of the party or one that your child loves.

For entertainment, you can include games, interactive activities, and crafts that match the theme of the party. You can also consider hiring a professional entertainer like a clown or a magician to keep the children entertained. You can also include a photo booth or a photo area to capture all the memories of the party.

Additionally, you can also consider incorporating a special activity or craft that your child can take home as a keepsake. This could be a handprint painting, a photo frame, or a special craft that they created during the party.

When it comes to the location, you can choose to have the party at home, in a park, or at a venue that caters to children's parties. Keep in mind that the location should be age-appropriate and have enough space for all the guests and activities.

As your child is now more independent, you can also consider involving them in the planning process. You can ask for their opinion on the theme, food, and activities. This will make them feel special and excited about their party.

Finally, do not forget to also consider the timing of the party, as a 3-year-old's attention span and energy levels may not be able to handle a long party. Also, consider hiring a professional photographer to capture all the memories of this special milestone.

In conclusion, planning and executing a 3rd birthday party can be a bit more complex than the previous years, but it also opens up new opportunities for themes, decorations, and activities. Remember to keep the guest list manageable, choose a theme that reflects your child's interests and personality, and include interactive elements and activities to keep the children entertained. With a little bit of planning, attention to detail and a lot of love, you'll be able to create a special and memorable celebration for your child.

CHAPTER FOUR
Four-ward to Fun!

The fourth birthday marks a significant milestone in your child's life as they are now in preschool and have a better understanding of the world around them. This means that your child's fourth birthday party should be geared towards interactive activities and games that foster learning and socialization.

When planning your child's fourth birthday party, it's important to keep in mind that your child is now more independent and may have specific interests or preferences. You can use this as an opportunity to plan a themed party that reflects your child's interests, while also incorporating educational elements. Popular themes for 4th birthday parties include: Space, Ocean, Farm and many more.

When it comes to decorations, you can be a bit more elaborate than the previous years, but still keep it age-appropriate. Balloons, streamers, and decorations that match the theme of the party are always a hit. You can also consider adding interactive elements like a scavenger hunt, a science station, or a craft station that related to the party's theme.

Food is still an important aspect of the party, and you can offer a mix of adult and kid-friendly food. You can also consider incorporating a candy buffet or a dessert table to add an extra special touch. The cake is still a significant part of the celebration, and you can choose a cake that matches the theme of the party or one that your child loves.

For entertainment, you can include games, interactive activities, and crafts that match the theme of the party and are also educational. You can also consider hiring a professional entertainer like a clown or a magician to keep the children entertained. You can also include a photo booth or a photo area to capture all the memories of the party.

Don't forget the party favors. You can choose favors that match the theme of the party or something that your child likes and that also relate to the party's theme. For example, if it's a Space-themed party, you can give out space-themed crafts or candies.

In terms of logistics, you can choose to have the party at home, in a park, or at a venue that caters to children's parties. Keep in mind that the location should be age-appropriate and have enough space for all the guests and activities. As your child is now more independent, you can also consider involving them in the planning process. You can ask for their opinion on the theme, food, and activities. This will make them feel special and excited about their party. Timing is also important for 4 years old, as they might get tired and overwhelmed quickly, plan accordingly. And don't forget to hire a professional photographer to capture all the memories of this special milestone.

Another important aspect to consider when planning your child's fourth birthday party is the inclusion of educational activities that cater to your child's developmental needs. At this age, children are starting to develop their cognitive and social skills, so incorporating activities that foster these skills can be beneficial. For example, you can include a station where children can practice their counting and matching skills or a station where children can practice their fine motor skills by assembling a puzzle or building with blocks.

Additionally, you can also consider incorporating a special activity or craft that your child can take home as a keepsake. This could be a handprint painting, a photo frame, or a special craft that they created during the party.

Finally, it is important to remember that the fourth birthday party should be a celebration of your child's growth and development. It is a time to come together with family and friends to celebrate and make memories that will last a lifetime. Make sure to have fun, enjoy the moment and don't stress too much about the small details, as the most important thing is that you and your child have a great time together.

CHAPTER FIVE
Five-tastic Friendship!

The fifth birthday is a special milestone for your child as they are now starting school and are becoming more independent. This means that your child's fifth birthday party should be geared towards interactive activities and games that foster teamwork and socialization.

When planning your child's fifth birthday party, it's important to keep in mind that your child is now more aware of their surroundings and may have specific interests or preferences. You can use this as an opportunity to plan a themed party that reflects your child's interests, while also incorporating teamwork-building elements. Popular themes for 5th birthday parties include: sports, adventure, and mystery.

When it comes to decorations, you can be a bit more elaborate than the previous years, but still keep it age-appropriate. Balloons, streamers, and decorations that match the theme of the party are always a hit. You can also consider adding interactive elements like a obstacle course, a treasure hunt, or a relay race that relates to the party's theme.

Food is still an important aspect of the party, and you can offer a mix of adult and kid-friendly food. You can also consider incorporating a candy buffet or a dessert table to add an extra special touch. The cake is still a significant part of the celebration, and you can choose a cake that matches the theme of the party or one that your child loves.

For entertainment, you can include games, interactive activities, and crafts that match the theme of the party and are also focused on teamwork-building. You can also consider hiring a professional entertainer like a clown or a magician to keep the children entertained. You can also include a photo booth or a photo area to capture all the memories of the party.

Don't forget the party favors. You can choose favors that match the theme of the party or something that your child likes and that also relate to the party's theme. For example, if it's a sports-themed party, you can give out mini sports equipment or candies.

In terms of logistics, you can choose to have the party at home, in a park, or at a venue that caters to children's parties. Keep in mind that the location should be age-appropriate and have enough space for all the guests and activities. As your child is now more independent, you can also consider involving them in the planning process. You can ask for their opinion on the theme, food, and activities. This will make them feel special and excited about their party. Timing is also important for 5 years old, as they might get tired and overwhelmed quickly, plan accordingly. And don't forget to hire a professional photographer to capture all the memories of this special milestone.

Another important aspect to consider when planning your child's fifth birthday party is the inclusion of teamwork-building activities that cater to your child's developmental needs. At this age, children are starting to develop their social skills and learn how to work in a group. Incorporating activities that foster teamwork can be beneficial. For example, you can include a station where children can work together to complete a puzzle or a station where children can play a group game like capture the flag.

Additionally, you can also consider incorporating a special activity or craft that your child can take home as a keepsake. This could be a handprint painting, a photo frame, or a special craft that they created during the party.

Finally, it is important to remember that the fifth birthday party should be a celebration of your child's growth and development. It is a time to come together with family and friends to celebrate and make memories that will last a lifetime. Make sure to have fun, enjoy the moment and don't stress too much about the small details, as the most important thing is that you and your child have a great time together and learn some valuable teamwork skills.

In conclusion, planning and executing a 5th birthday party can be a bit more complex than the previous years, but it also opens up new opportunities for themes, decorations, and activities that foster teamwork and socialization. Remember to keep the guest list manageable, choose a theme that reflects your child's interests and personality, and include interactive elements and activities that promote teamwork and socialization. With a little bit of planning, attention to detail and a lot of love, you'll be able to create a special and memorable celebration for your child that will also help them learn valuable teamwork skills.

CHAPTER SIX
Six-travagant Creativity

The sixth birthday is a special milestone for your child as they are now in the first grade and are starting to develop their own sense of self. This means that your child's sixth birthday party should be geared towards interactive activities and games that foster creativity and self-expression.

When planning your child's sixth birthday party, it's important to keep in mind that your child is now more aware of their own interests and may have specific preferences. You can use this as an opportunity to plan a themed party that reflects your child's interests, while also incorporating creative elements. Popular themes for 6th birthday parties include: art, magic, and mystery.

When it comes to decorations, you can be a bit more elaborate than the previous years, but still keep it age-appropriate. Balloons, streamers, and decorations that match the theme of the party are always a hit. You can also consider adding interactive elements like an art station, a magic show, or a mystery-solving game that relate to the party's theme.

Food is still an important aspect of the party, and you can offer a mix of adult and kid-friendly food. You can also consider incorporating a candy buffet or a dessert table to add an extra special touch. The cake is still a significant part of the celebration, and you can choose a cake that matches the theme of the party or one that your child loves.

For entertainment, you can include games, interactive activities, and crafts that match the theme of the party and are also focused on creativity and self-expression. You can also consider hiring a professional entertainer like a clown or a magician to keep the children entertained. You can also include a photo booth or a photo area to capture all the memories of the party.

Don't forget the party favors. You can choose favors that match the theme of the party or something that your child likes and that also relate to the party's theme. For example, if it's an art-themed party, you can give out art supplies or candies.

In terms of logistics, you can choose to have the party at home, in a park, or at a venue that caters to children's parties. Keep in mind that the location should be age-appropriate and have enough space for all the guests and activities. As your child is now more independent, you can also consider involving them in the planning process. You can ask for their opinion on the theme, food, and activities. This will make them feel special and excited about their party. Timing is also important for 6 years old, as they might get tired and overwhelmed quickly, plan accordingly. And don't forget to hire a professional photographer to capture all the memories of this special milestone.

Another important aspect to consider when planning your child's sixth birthday party is the inclusion of creative activities that cater to your child's developmental needs. At this age, children are starting to develop their own sense of self and interests. Incorporating activities that foster creativity and self-expression can be beneficial. For example, you can include a station where children can create their own art or a station where children can perform a magic show.

Additionally, you can also consider incorporating a special activity or craft that your child can take home as a keepsake. This could be a handprint painting, a photo frame, or a special craft that they created during the party.

Finally, it is important to remember that the sixth birthday party should be a celebration of your child's growth and development. It is a time to come together with family and friends to celebrate and make memories that will last a lifetime. Make sure to have fun, enjoy the moment and don't stress too much about the small details, as the most important thing is that you and your child have a great time together and learn some valuable self-expression and creativity skills.

CHAPTER SEVEN
Seven-sational Success!

The seventh birthday is a special milestone for your child as they are now in the second grade and are becoming more independent. This means that your child's seventh birthday party should be geared towards interactive activities and games that foster teamwork and socialization.

When planning your child's seventh birthday party, it's important to keep in mind that your child is now more aware of their own interests and may have specific preferences. You can use this as an opportunity to plan a themed party that reflects your child's interests, while also incorporating teamwork-building elements. Popular themes for 7th birthday parties include: adventure, mystery, and science.

When it comes to decorations, you can be a bit more elaborate than the previous years, but still keep it age-appropriate. Balloons, streamers, and decorations that match the theme of the party are always a hit. You can also consider adding interactive elements like an obstacle course, a treasure hunt, or a relay race that relates to the party's theme.

Food is still an important aspect of the party, and you can offer a mix of adult and kid-friendly food. You can also consider incorporating a candy buffet or a dessert table to add an extra special touch. The cake is still a significant part of the celebration, and you can choose a cake that matches the theme of the party or one that your child loves.

For entertainment, you can include games, interactive activities, and crafts that match the theme of the party and are also focused on teamwork-building. You can also consider hiring a professional entertainer like a clown or a magician to keep the children entertained. You can also include a photo booth or a photo area to capture all the memories of the party.

Don't forget the party favors. You can choose favors that match the theme of the party or something that your child likes and that also relate to the party's theme. For example, if it's an adventure-themed party, you can give out mini binoculars or candies.

In terms of logistics, you can choose to have the party at home, in a park, or at a venue that caters to children's parties. Keep in mind that the location should be age-appropriate and have enough space for all the guests and activities. As your child is now more independent, you can also consider involving them in the planning process. You can ask for their opinion on the theme, food, and activities. This will make them feel special and excited about their party. Timing is also important for 7 years old, as they might get tired and overwhelmed quickly, plan accordingly. And don't forget to hire a professional photographer to capture all the memories of this special milestone.

Another important aspect to consider when planning your child's seventh birthday party is the inclusion of teamwork-building activities that cater to your child's developmental needs. At this age, children are starting to develop their social skills and learn how to work in a group. Incorporating activities that foster teamwork can be beneficial. For example, you can include a station where children can work together to complete a puzzle or a station where children can play a group game like capture the flag.

Additionally, you can also consider incorporating a special activity or craft that your child can take home as a keepsake. This could be a handprint painting, a photo frame, or a special craft that they created during the party.

Finally, it is important to remember that the seventh birthday party should be a celebration of your child's growth and development. It is a time to come together with family and friends to celebrate and make memories that will last a lifetime. Make sure to have fun, enjoy the moment and don't stress too much about the small details, as the most important thing is that you and your child have a great time together and learn some valuable teamwork skills.

In conclusion, planning and executing a 7th birthday party can be a bit more complex than the previous years, but it also opens up new opportunities for themes, decorations, and activities that foster teamwork and socialization. Remember to keep the guest list manageable, choose a theme that reflects your child's interests and personality, and include interactive elements and activities that promote teamwork and socialization. With a little bit of planning, attention to detail and a lot of love, you'll be able to create a special and memorable celebration for your child that will also help them learn valuable teamwork skills.

CHAPTER EIGHT
Eighth-Year Extravaganza

The eighth birthday is a special milestone for your child as they are now in the third grade and are becoming more independent and confident. This means that your child's eighth birthday party should be geared towards interactive activities and games that foster creativity, self-expression and teamwork.

When planning your child's eighth birthday party, it's important to keep in mind that your child is now more aware of their own interests and may have specific preferences. You can use this as an opportunity to plan a themed party that reflects your child's interests, while also incorporating teamwork-building and creativity elements. Popular themes for 8th birthday parties include: movie night, game night, and sport-themed.

When it comes to decorations, you can be a bit more elaborate than the previous years, but still keep it age-appropriate. Balloons, streamers, and decorations that match the theme of the party are always a hit. You can also consider adding interactive elements like a photo booth, a karaoke station or a DIY station that relates to the party's theme.

Food is still an important aspect of the party, and you can offer a mix of adult and kid-friendly food. You can also consider incorporating a candy buffet or a dessert table to add an extra special touch. The cake is still a significant part of the celebration, and you can choose a cake that matches the theme of the party or one that your child loves.

For entertainment, you can include games, interactive activities, and crafts that match the theme of the party and are also focused on teamwork-building, creativity and self-expression. You can also consider hiring a professional entertainer like a DJ or a magician to keep the children entertained. You can also include a photo booth or a photo area to capture all the memories of the party.

Don't forget the party favors. You can choose favors that match the theme of the party or something that your child likes and that also relate to the party's theme. For example, if it's a movie night themed party, you can give out popcorn boxes or movie-themed candies. If it's a sports-themed party, you can give out mini sports equipment or team-themed candies.

In terms of logistics, you can choose to have the party at home, in a park, or at a venue that caters to children's parties. Keep in mind that the location should be age-appropriate and have enough space for all the guests and activities. As your child is now more independent, you can also consider involving them in the planning process. You can ask for their opinion on the theme, food, and activities. This will make them feel special and excited about their party. Timing is also important for 8 years old, as they might get tired and overwhelmed quickly, plan accordingly. And don't forget to hire a professional photographer to capture all the memories of this special milestone.

Another important aspect to consider when planning your child's eighth birthday party is the inclusion of activities that cater to your child's developmental needs. At this age, children are starting to develop their own sense of self and interests. Incorporating activities that foster creativity, self-expression and teamwork can be beneficial. For example, you can include a station where children can create their own movie or a station where children can play a group game like capture the flag.

Finally, it is important to remember that the eighth birthday party should be a celebration of your child's growth and development. It is a time to come together with family and friends to celebrate and make memories that will last a lifetime. Make sure to have fun, enjoy the moment and don't stress too much about the small details, as the most important thing is that you and your child have a great time together and learn some valuable teamwork, self-expression and creativity skills.

CHAPTER NINE
Ninth-Birthday Bliss

The ninth birthday is a special milestone for your child as they are now in the fourth grade and are becoming more independent and confident. This means that your child's ninth birthday party should be geared towards interactive activities and games that foster creativity, self-expression, teamwork, and physical activity.

When planning your child's ninth birthday party, it's important to keep in mind that your child is now more aware of their own interests and may have specific preferences. You can use this as an opportunity to plan a themed party that reflects your child's interests, while also incorporating teamwork-building, creativity, self-expression and physical activity elements. Popular themes for 9th birthday parties include: science, adventure and mystery.

When it comes to decorations, you can be a bit more elaborate than the previous years, but still keep it age-appropriate. Balloons, streamers, and decorations that match the theme of the party are always a hit. You can also consider adding interactive elements like a science experiment station, a treasure hunt, or a relay race that relates to the party's theme.

Food is still an important aspect of the party, and you can offer a mix of adult and kid-friendly food. You can also consider incorporating a candy buffet or a dessert table to add an extra special touch. The cake is still a significant part of the celebration, and you can choose a cake that matches the theme of the party or one that your child loves.

For entertainment, you can include games, interactive activities, and crafts that match the theme of the party and are also focused on teamwork-building, creativity, self-expression and physical activity. You can also consider hiring a professional entertainer like a scientist or a magician to keep the children entertained. You can also include a photo booth or a photo area to capture all the memories of the party.

Don't forget the party favors. You can choose favors that match the theme of the party or something that your child likes and that also relate to the party's theme. For example, if it's a science-themed party, you can give out mini telescopes or candies. If it's an adventure-themed party, you can give out mini binoculars or compass.

In terms of logistics, you can choose to have the party at home, in a park, or at a venue that caters to children's parties. Keep in mind that the location should be age-appropriate and have enough space for all the guests and activities. As your child is now more independent, you can also consider involving them in the planning process. You can ask for their opinion on the theme, food, and activities. This will make them feel special and excited about their party. Timing is also important for 9 years old, as they have a lot of energy and need to move around, plan accordingly. And don't forget to hire a professional photographer to capture all the memories of this special milestone.

Another important aspect to consider when planning your child's ninth birthday party is the inclusion of activities that cater to your child's developmental needs. At this age, children are starting to develop their own sense of self and interests. Incorporating activities that foster creativity, self-expression, teamwork, and physical activity can be beneficial. For example, you can include a station where children can make their own science experiment or a station where children can play a group game like capture the flag.

Finally, it is important to remember that the ninth birthday party should be a celebration of your child's growth and development. It is a time to come together with family and friends to celebrate and make memories that will last a lifetime. Make sure to have fun, enjoy the moment and don't stress too much about the small details, as the most important thing is that you and your child have a great time together and learn some valuable teamwork, self-expression, creativity and physical activity skills.

CHAPTER TEN
Tenth Birthday Adventures

The tenth birthday is a special milestone for your child as they are now in the fifth grade and are becoming more independent and confident. This means that your child's tenth birthday party should be geared towards interactive activities and games that foster creativity, self-expression, teamwork, physical activity and responsibility.

When planning your child's tenth birthday party, it's important to keep in mind that your child is now more aware of their own interests and may have specific preferences. You can use this as an opportunity to plan a themed party that reflects your child's interests, while also incorporating teamwork-building, creativity, self-expression, physical activity and responsibility elements. Popular themes for 10th birthday parties include: carnival, adventure and mystery.

When it comes to decorations, you can be a bit more elaborate than the previous years, but still keep it age-appropriate. Balloons, streamers, and decorations that match the theme of the party are always a hit. You can also consider adding interactive elements like a carnival games station, a treasure hunt, or a relay race that relates to the party's theme.

Food is still an important aspect of the party, and you can offer a mix of adult and kid-friendly food. You can also consider incorporating a candy buffet or a dessert table to add an extra special touch. The cake is still a significant part of the celebration, and you can choose a cake that matches the theme of the party or one that your child loves.

For entertainment, you can include games, interactive activities, and crafts that match the theme of the party and are also focused on teamwork-building, creativity, self-expression, physical activity and responsibility. You can also consider hiring a professional entertainer like a clown or a magician to keep the children entertained. You can also include a photo booth or a photo area to capture all the memories of the party.

Don't forget the party favors. You can choose favors that match the theme of the party or something that your child likes and that also relate to the party's theme. For example, if it's a carnival-themed party, you can give out mini stuffed animals or candies. If it's an adventure-themed party, you can give out mini compasses or a flashlight.

In terms of logistics, you can choose to have the party at home, in a park, or at a venue that caters to children's parties. Keep in mind that the location should be age-appropriate and have enough space for all the guests and activities. As your child is now more independent, you can also consider involving them in the planning process. You can ask for their opinion on the theme, food, and activities. This will make them feel special and excited about their party. Timing is also important for 10 years old, as they have a lot of energy and need to move around, plan accordingly. And don't forget to hire a professional photographer to capture all the memories of this special milestone.

Another important aspect to consider when planning your child's tenth birthday party is the inclusion of activities that cater to your child's developmental needs. At this age, children are starting to develop their own sense of self and interests. Incorporating activities that foster creativity, self-expression, teamwork, physical activity and responsibility can be beneficial. For example, you can include a station where children can make their own carnival games or a station where children can play a group game like capture the flag.

Finally, it is important to remember that the tenth birthday party should be a celebration of your child's growth and development. It is a time to come together with family and friends to celebrate and make memories that will last a lifetime. Make sure to have fun, enjoy the moment and don't stress too much about the small details, as the most important thing is that you and your child have a great time together and learn some valuable teamwork, self-expression, creativity, physical activity and responsibility skills.

Epilogue

As I sit here and reflect on all the birthday parties I've planned and executed for my three children over the years, I am filled with a sense of nostalgia and pride. From my oldest child's first birthday party, where we were still figuring out the ropes of parenthood, to my youngest child's tenth birthday party, where we watched our baby grow into a responsible young person, each party has been a unique and special experience.

I remember the excitement of planning my oldest child's first birthday party, the joy of seeing my second child's face light up as he discovered the treasure hunt we had planned for his fourth birthday party and the pride of watching my youngest child take the lead in planning her tenth birthday party. Each party has been a celebration of my child's growth and development, and I am grateful to have been a part of it.

As a mother, planning birthday parties has taught me many valuable lessons. I've learned that every child is unique and has their own interests and preferences. I've learned that each age comes with its own set of challenges and opportunities. And most importantly, I've learned that a well-planned party can be a wonderful way to celebrate a child's growth and development while fostering creativity, self-expression, teamwork, physical activity and responsibility.

I hope that this book has been helpful in providing inspiration and guidance for planning your child's birthday parties. Remember to have fun, enjoy the moment, and don't stress too much about the small details. The most important thing is that you and your child have a great time together and make memories that will last a lifetime.

As you plan and execute your child's birthday parties, I encourage you to take a step back and enjoy the journey. Cherish the little moments and the big milestones, and don't be afraid to make

mistakes. These parties are not just about the party itself, but also about the memories and the bond that you will create with your child.
Thank you for joining me on this journey, and I wish you all the best as you plan and execute birthday parties for your own children. Happy planning and happy birthday!

www.ingramcontent.com/pod-product-compliance
Lightning Source LLC
LaVergne TN
LVHW020544160826
845677LV00015B/4188